Little Stars

Little Stars
SOCCER

A CRABTREE SEEDLINGS BOOK

Taylor Farley

CRABTREE
PUBLISHING COMPANY
WWW.CRABTREEBOOKS.COM

I am on a **soccer** team.

Shin guards protect our legs.

We wear shin
guards under
our socks.

Cleats help us grip the ground and make fast turns.

We play on a
soccer field.

goal

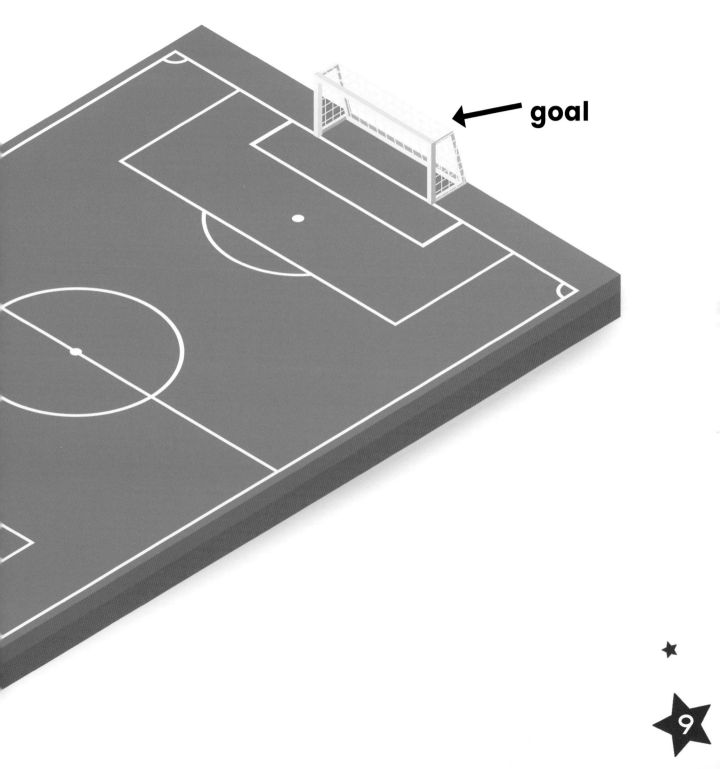

goal

9

We do warm-up exercises before each game.

The referee makes sure we follow the rules.

We kick, **dribble**, and pass the ball.

Each team tries to get the ball into the other team's net.

goalkeeper

The **goalkeeper** guards the **goal** and tries to stop the ball from going in.

The team that scores the most goals wins.

Glossary

cleats (KLEETS): Cleats are sports shoes that have spikes or bumps on their soles.

dribble (DRIB-uhl): When you dribble a soccer ball, you control and move it with short kicks or nudges with your foot.

goal (GOHL): A goal is scored when a player gets the ball into the other team's net. The soccer net with its frame is also called a goal.

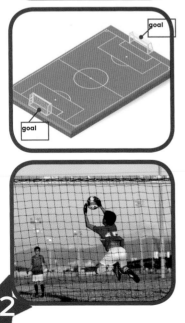

goalkeeper (GOHL keep-ur): The goalkeeper's job is to keep the ball out of the net.

shin guards (SHIN GARDZ): Shin guards are pads worn under the socks to protect the player's shins.

soccer (SOK-ur): Soccer is a game played with two teams. Each team tries to get the ball into the other team's net to score a goal.

Index

School-to-Home Support for Caregivers and Teachers

Crabtree Seedlings books help children grow by letting them practice reading. Here are a few guiding questions to help the reader build his or her comprehension skills. Possible answers are included.

Before Reading

- **What do I think this book is about?** I think this book is about playing soccer. It might tell us about the rules of a soccer game.

- **What do I want to learn about this topic?** I want to learn about the clothing and equipment that soccer players wear.

During Reading

- **I wonder why...** I wonder why the referee holds a yellow card in the picture on page 13.

- **What have I learned so far?** I learned that soccer players wear shin guards to protect their legs and cleats to help them grip the ground. They wear uniforms too.

After Reading

- **What details did I learn about this topic?** I learned that soccer players follow rules. They listen to the referee.

- **Write down unfamiliar words and ask questions to help understand their meaning.** I see the word *dribble* on page 15 and the word *goalkeeper* on page 19. The other vocabulary words are listed on pages 22 and 23.

Library and Archives Canada Cataloguing in Publication

Title: Little stars soccer / Taylor Farley.
Other titles: Soccer
Names: Farley, Taylor, author.
Description: Series statement: Little stars | "A Crabtree seedlings book". | Includes index. |
Previously published in electronic format by Blue Door Education in 2020.
Identifiers: Canadiana 20200379798 | ISBN 9781427129871 (hardcover) | ISBN 9781427130051 (softcover)
Subjects: LCSH: Soccer—Juvenile literature.
Classification: LCC GV943.25 .F37 2021 | DDC j796.334—dc23

Library of Congress Cataloging-in-Publication Data

Names: Farley, Taylor, author.
Title: Little stars soccer / Taylor Farley.
Other titles: Soccer
Description: New York, NY : Crabtree Publishing Company, [2021] | Series: Little stars: a Crabtree seedlings book | Includes index.
Identifiers: LCCN 2020049305 | ISBN 9781427129871 (hardcover) | ISBN 9781427130051 (paperback)
Subjects: LCSH: Soccer--Juvenile literature.
Classification: LCC GV943.25 .F36 2021 | DDC 796.334--dc23
LC record available at https://lccn.loc.gov/2020049305

Crabtree Publishing Company

www.crabtreebooks.com   1–800–387–7650

Written by Taylor Farley

Production coordinator and Prepress technician: Samara Parent

Print coordinator: Katherine Berti

e-book ISBN 978-0-998148-72-4

Print book version produced jointly with Blue Door Education in 2021

Printed in the U.S.A./012021/CG20201102

Photo credits: Cover © Fotokostic; page 2-3 © Tumarkin Igor - ITPS; page 4 © MaZiKab; page 4-5 © Bull's-Eye Arts; page 6-7 © Pedro Monteiro; page 8-9 © GarikProst; page 10-11 g Fotokostic; page 12-13 © bikeriderlondon; page 14-15 © Nirat.pix; page 16-17 © Vladimir57; page 18-19 © leon58; page 21 © Monkey Business Images; page 22 middle photo © Vladimir57. All photos from Shutterstock.com

Published in Canada
Crabtree Publishing
616 Welland Ave.
St. Catharines, Ontario
L2M 5V6

Published in the United States
Crabtree Publishing
347 Fifth Ave.
Suite 1402-145
New York, NY 10016

Published in the United Kingdom
Crabtree Publishing
Maritime House
Basin Road North, Hove
BN41 1WR

Published in Australia
Crabtree Publishing
Unit 3 – 5 Currumbin Court
Capalaba
QLD 4157